Shipping Container Homes

The Ultimate Beginners Guide to Designing, Building & Investing in Shipping Container Homes

Copyright 2015 by Gregory Moto - All rights reserved.

This document is geared towards providing exact and reliable information in regards to the topic and issue covered. The publication is sold with the idea that the publisher is not required to render accounting, officially permitted, or otherwise, qualified services. If advice is necessary, legal or professional, a practiced individual in the profession should be ordered.

- From a Declaration of Principles which was accepted and approved equally by a Committee of the American Bar Association and a Committee of Publishers and Associations.
In no way is it legal to reproduce, duplicate, or transmit any part of this document in either electronic means or in printed format. Recording of this publication is strictly prohibited and any storage of this document is not allowed unless with written permission from the publisher. All rights reserved.

The information provided herein is stated to be truthful and consistent, in that any liability, in terms of inattention or otherwise, by any usage or abuse of any policies, processes, or directions contained within is the solitary and utter responsibility of the recipient reader. Under no circumstances will any legal responsibility or blame be held against the publisher for any reparation, damages, or monetary loss due to the information herein, either directly or indirectly. Respective authors own all copyrights not held by the publisher.

The information herein is offered for informational purposes solely, and is universal as so. The presentation of the information is without contract or any type of guarantee assurance.

The trademarks that are used are without any consent, and the publication of the trademark is without permission or backing by the trademark owner. All trademarks and brands within this book are for clarifying purposes only and are the owned by the owners themselves, not affiliated with this document.

Contents

What are Shipping Containers?

The view from a shipping container yard where empty and loaded steel cargo units are kept for safety until their next voyage. (Image from photography.nationalgeographic.com)

There are three main purposes that shipping containers serve to satisfy. They are meant to withstand heavy loads of shipment, product storage, and excessive handling without much of a hassle. It is with these reasons in mind that these cargo containers are built to last; to be as strong and durable as possible so as not to succumb to wear and tear early in their life. There are different types of shipping containers and these come in varying sizes as well. Most common are the steel boxes which can be used over and over again and then there are those which are meant for short term reliability, the corrugated boxes. The former is utilized for what is known as intermodal shipping. It basically means that the container has been designed to be moved or transported from one location to another without having to be unloaded not to mention repacked. Here are some shipping container types that are commonplace in the importation and exportation industry.

- Crates

A crate is just like a wooden box container but much larger in overall dimension. It is ideal for transporting heavy items including those which carry an awkward shape. It is created to offer an internal structure that is self-supporting easily increasing the protection for whatever contents are placed within.

- Wooden Boxes

Wooden box containers are similar to the corrugated variety in the sense that they are ideal for short-term use but the former is more durable and can withstand much more wear and tear over time. They can also be used to transport heavier not to mention denser loads. Some of the common uses for the wooden boxes include government or military shipments, artillery, and wine freight.

Wooden boxes and crates were some of the most widely used if not most popular forms of shipping containers centuries ago. These were the predecessors of modern day modular shipping containers. (Image from www.newrailwaymodellers.co.uk)

- Corrugated Boxes

Corrugated box containers are normally made from fiberboard and are popular options for product transport. Strong and quite durable but ideal for short-term use, these ensure the safe transport of various loads from points A to B. The material used in making them is lightweight easily saving costs on shipment weight and the like. Even if it is ideal for short-term use, this really does not cause problems for importers or exporters as the fiberboard is highly recyclable. There isn't much waste generated from these container boxes.

- Pails

In some cases, standard pails or buckets are used to transport products across countries. Pails made out of steel or plastic can be used to transport granular and fluid materials.

- Unit Load Devices

When materials need to specifically be transported by aircraft, there is only one type of container that can be used to house them in and this is the ULD or unit load device. It is the same steel container used to carry luggage on commercial flights. Apart from passenger luggage, these containers are often used to carry mail or freight and are designed to fit the narrow structures of planes. When ULDs are used, different types of cargo are normally fitted into single units until they are filled to the brim to save space on board. Doing so allows aircrafts to carry as much load as they can without having to worry about having tons of units on the plane. Fewer units to load and unload allows for a reduction in losses or flight delays. Ground control always has a packing manifest to maintain organization. Each unit also has the necessary tracking information.

Unit load devices as seen in a sample aircraft cross-section. These containers are specifically designed to fit snugly in cargo planes or underneath the passenger area of commercial airlines. (Image from www.datab.us)

- Drum Shippers

Drum shippers, usually fabricated from steel, may also be made out of fiber or plastic depending on the intended purpose. Aside from carrying granular products, these also work perfectly in storing and transporting fluids.

- Bulk Boxes

A box container, also referred to as a bulk bin, is used to ship materials in bulk quantities. It is usually made in the same size as a standard pallet.

- Intermodal Freight Shipping Containers

Aside from domestic transport, other locational transport needs for various products including those done from country to country are satisfied by intermodal freight shipping containers. There are millions of these cargo units around the world, some of which are in active transit, others stored in warehouses, and others reused in various ways. When it comes to long-distance freight done on a global scale, these shipping containers play very important roles. Although these are extremely dependable, sending them back to their points of origin can be costly. It is cheaper to simply source new ones should the need for such a container arise. This is why most of these intermodal containers are discarded, to save costs on the return trip. The improvement of intercontinental trade can be attributed to the invention of these cargo containers. Not only have they been able to help reduce transport costs but they also helped prevent losses from product damage and losses.

- Intermediate Bulk Shipping Containers

Known in the industry as IBCs, intermediate bulk containers are primarily used to transport fluid products and other bulk materials. Because of these contents, the containers are commonly fabricated from a durable plastic material. In some cases, these can also be made from other materials like composite metals or steel. A special feature offered by an IBC is its collapsibility allowing for easier storage after it is used while awaiting the next shipment.

A spin-off to the standard IBC is the FIBC which stands for flexible intermediate bulk container. Unlike its box-type counterparts, an FIBC is used to describe freight containers which come in the form of a bulk bag or large sack. It is ideal for the storage and effective transport of products that have a granular nature like rice, grains, beads, and the like. Most of the time, burlap fabric is used to make these but there are those which use a synthetic material woven into bags. In some cases, to ensure that no moisture seeps into the bags and ruins its contents, the bags are dipped into a sealing agent prior to use.

- Insulated Shipping Containers

There are companies which engage in the trade of products which are temperature sensitive like ice cream, frozen goods, and the like. In this case, what they rely on are insulated shipping containers. These are equipped with cooling systems that ensure all products maintain their freshness while in transport up until delivery.

Aside from having a special internal coating which ensures that the temperature is kept at a certain temperature, air vents where cooling systems can be installed are all part of an insulated shipping container. It is similar to having a gigantic thermos in tow. (Image from www.shipping-container-housing.com)

- Specialized Shipping Containers

Specialized carriers work primarily by transporting weaponry by road, rail, or sea. These custom-made containers can also be used to transport aviation materials. Aside from the necessary cushioning and support pegs, the internal structure is also built to have sufficient bracing. Outside are carrying handles, support lift rings, and locks.

When the phrase specialized shipping container is used, it can also pertain to extenders for other shipping containers. For example, there is something known as a high cube container. What this does is provide an extra foot on the top of a standard cargo unit. There are similar extenders that may also add a foot or two across all walls of a shipping container box. The steel tanks commonly seen transporting gasoline and other fuel by-products are other examples of specialized shipping containers.

- Transit Shipping Cases

Transit shipping cases serve a more distinct purpose and this is to carry audio-visual equipment like cameras. They have reinforced edges to ensure that the fragile contents are always safe while in transport. The interior is also lined with the necessary support pegs and cushions to keep everything in place.

- Road Transport Cases

Road cases are the black carrying cases normally used to transport musical instruments not to mention theater props. The external structure is tough yet there is an internal fabric lining usually made out of velvet. Adequate cushioning or padding moulded to the form of its contents help secure the objects in place.

How are Steel Shipping Containers Made?

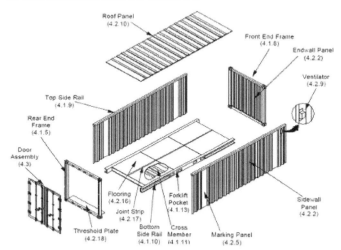

This diagram shows the individual panel structures that go into one modular shipping container unit. (Image from www.residentialshippingcontainerprimer.com)

Shipping containers are known for being highly durable with the most popular variety being those made out of heavy duty steel. There is always the question on why these boxes are so strong and what makes them such and the answer is simple. These cargo units are extremely strong because of the metal composite that they have been fabricated from. Because they are designed to withstand the elements not to mention heavy loads, and because they are meant to be used and reused over time, a special kind of steel material, Corten, is used.

Corten is a type of steel component often referred to as weathering steel. The material, when exposed to the elements, allows light rust to form on the surface. To most, this might not seem to be the best thing but the light rust actually acts as a secondary barrier or armor, which strengthens the steel over time. The rust does not progress to the degree, which eats at the metal. In this case, it is more of an ally to the steel rather than an enemy. Aside from shipping containers, this material is also used to reinforce bridges, towers, chimneys, sculptures, and rail cars to name a few.

Every time a shipping container is made, manufacturers line the Corten walls with marine grade paint that acts as a sealant and protective coating. Over time, the paint will degrade due to wear and tear. It is during this time when the material starts promulgating the formation of light rust, which replaces the paint as the structure's external protection.

A Deeper Look into Intermodal Shipping Containers

Intermodal shipping containers are some of the most widely used cargo units around the world. These are made out of a steel composite and come in various types not to mention sizes. A huge chunk of the total number of available shipping containers around the globe are referred to as dry freight which basically means that they are general purpose containers used to transport different dry materials or products across continents. These durable steel boxes come with double-ended doors that can be closed and sealed with ease. The standard lengths are either twenty or forty feet with a height ranging from eight and a half to nine and a half feet. If necessary, an extender can be added to the top wall offering an additional foot of height per container.

Intermodal shipping containers can be transported from storage yard to trucks, trains, or ships with the use of lifting cranes. (Image from www.shippingcontainerliving.com)

An intermodal shipping container is one of the larger shipping boxes readily available today and is designed to cater to intermodal transport. It means that these boxes can be shipped via different modes of transportation including land, air, and sea. Aside from this, the containers can be shipped without having to unload or reload cargo until they reach their final destination. Securing the boxes is easy as there are multiple locking systems in each one with the final keys only available to the shipper or receiver.

Similar to how pallets and cardboard boxes function, these kinds of shipping containers are ideal for bundling cargo into an easy-to-handle package. The containers can easily be moved using lifters or cranes, they can neatly be placed side by side, and they can also be stacked atop one another. Aside from easy transport, this also allows for organized storage. All of these capabilities, together with the individual identifying marks and details per container unit, can be attributed to several key construction features applied to these shipping containers.

Millions of these intermodal cargo units can be found around the world actively being used in the constant importation and exportation of goods and materials. Years after their inception, they have become the primary choice for carrying cargo as they allow for more effective and efficient transport. For a twenty footer, it weighs an average of 2200 kg empty and can handle a content load of 28200 kg for a final net allowable load of 30400 kg. The forty footer can handle the same net weight but weighs more when empty, around 3800 kg which means the maximum internal load it can handle is about 26600 kg.

In the case of stacking, without additional

support pillars, standard forty footers can be stacked one on top of the other. Without modifications, it is not safe to stack containers not of the same size on top of the other. For twenty footers, it can only hold a second storey forty footer if there are two twenty footers side by side supporting the load. It is always best to consult a structural engineer when it comes to something like this to ensure that the structure is balanced and safe for whatever purpose it intends to serve.

When in transport or while in storage, shipping container units can be stacked on top of each other. They are secured in place not only by the corner supports but additional linking mechanisms as well. (Image from www.londonshippingcontainers.co.uk)

How Intermodal Shipping Containers Came to Light

It was during the early part of the 1800s when cargo transport by rail gained widespread popularity. During this time, cross-continent shipments were already being catered to and railways were followed by efficient sea transport options. The United Kingdom stood as the center of all these and it was in the UK where the concept of timber shipping boxes originated. The structures were built using a steel frame with outer walls and flooring created out of wood. It was a hundred years later when the prototype for the first all-steel cargo unit would come out.

There was a time when rail freight shipping was all the rage but the industry needed help when the economy fell. This was when more efficient and secure forms of shipping containers were developed. (Image from en.wikipedia.org)

It was the Bureau International des Containers et du Transport Intermodal or IBC during the early 1900s that established the primary standard for shipping containers at a time when a majority of transport routes ran through Europe. In other parts of the world, there was no existing standard. Containers did not offer their stackable feature yet. Originally, shipping containers were created to help rail companies combat the effects of the economic downfall as a result of the Wall Street crash which occurred in the Big Apple in 1929.

As a way of marketing these revolutionary container systems to other parts of Europe and the United States as well, a joint effort from the Swiss Museum of Transport and the Bureau International des Containers or BIC led to a live presentation of various container systems to representatives from the shipping industry. It took place at the railway station of Zürich Tiefenbrunnen on April 1951. The different designs were meant to satisfy the different needs of nations. The presentation led to the selection of distinct systems for each cluster of countries. The most popular system was the Laadkisten, which means loading bins when translated. These were the first containers to use rolling loading systems. It is the predecessor of the current steel shipping container units that are being used today.

It was during the 1940s when the use of these steel shipping containers became widespread thanks in part to the United States military and commercial shipping businesses that actually manufactured similar units in-house. It was the

US Army that developed the idea to put corrugations on the steel walls to increase durability without having to increase the amount of steel needed for the structure. It was also the first type of container to have double end doors and improved on the rolling structure first applied to the Laadkisten unit. This particular shipping container unit was shared with other countries like Korea for example where it was successfully used for commercial purposes. The US Army's container prototype was later improved upon with the new version having the well-known stacking feature.

The United States military would ship artillery, weapons, prepackaged sustenance, and other essential items in specialized steel shipping containers. (Image from www.youtube.com)

As the years progressed, engineers continued their work to improve the design and function of the intermodal shipping container. They were made to last longer and be more reliable in the safe transportation of various products across different channels. When the 1970s arrived, a specific set of standards applicable on a global scale was established for these containers allowing for consistent transporting, loading, and unloading of goods across different ports. By having one set of standards for everybody, transport became more efficient saving everyone lots of time and money. These days, intermodal shipping containers continue to be used around the world but they carry an additional purpose and that is to stand as structural blocks for residences and other livable shelters.

Introduction to Shipping Container Homes

There are different kinds of homes available these days varying on structural design, materials used, and the overall dimensions employed. Usually, homeowners choose a style of house based on personal design preferences, sustainability, and of course, their budget. There are certain types of homes that are more expensive to construct than others and oftentimes require a larger parcel of land to be constructed in. Some allow for a DIY approach while others call for no less than a professional team of workers from contractors to architects to landscapers.

Modular containers, once serving the sole purpose of product transport, can now be used architecturally as building blocks for amazingly efficient and aesthetically beautiful homes. (Image from www.homedsgn.com)

With housing markets currently in a volatile state and with home prices rising every passing year, people who are interested in home ownership rather than rentals are becoming more innovative in their choice of shelter. One mode of housing that is increasingly becoming popular makes use of shipping containers for its base structure. Indeed shipping container homes have grown to become a more affordable, cost-effective, sustainable, and unique form of housing.

Different countries across continents regularly make use of shipping containers to satisfy their importation and exportation needs. These cargo units are built from reinforced steel allowing them to function despite exposure to harsh weather conditions and heavy loads not to mention rough handling across ports. These are used to transport various products on land, sea, and air. To satisfy their primary purpose, they are manufactured in such a way that durability is never an issue thereby making them excellent structures for makeshift houses.

Thousands if not millions of these containers are regularly manufactured every year to cater to a growing demand. Homeowners interested in having a shipping container home of their own can buy them new or second hand. Regardless of their quality, these are always available to those who need them and the price tag for the pre-fabricated structure is relatively cheap compared to having to build one from scratch when constructing a house.

Not only is the cost rather enticing but using these containers make for a greener approach to homebuilding as well. When old units are bought for the purpose of building a house, the steel is recycled without having to exert additional effort or burn through resources to melt it down. It significantly reduces one's carbon footprint adding to its appeal for new age homeowners.

Although the space a shipping container provides can be quite limited, it has the feature of being open to modifications. A comfortable house can easily be made by combining several of these containers vertically or horizontally. Homeowners who can survive without that much space can even build a house from a single unit without much of a hassle. Because the structure has already been pre-fabricated, DIY-ers, provided that they are skilled handymen, have the ability to construct container homes without the need for professional assistance further dropping their construction costs.

There are more things to shipping container homes than what the eyes can see. They have their fair share of pros and cons. Different elements go into the construction process.

Various costs come with this type of project and so on and so forth. Reading on, you will find out more about these container units, how they function, and how they can readily be used to create a one-of-a-kind home. You will also learn about important steps and guidelines that will help you build a shipping container home properly enabling you to save on costs and preventing the onset of structural problems as time passes.

Advantages of Shipping Container Homes

Just a single unit is enough to provide ample space for a homeowner. With a minimalist design, it can easily be transformed into an awe-inspiring residential palace. (Image from www.crystalmoondesign.ca)

Each structure carries its own set of pros and cons and shipping container homes are not exempt from this. The concept is fairly new and there currently exists a specialized niche market for these structures. A growing number of homeowners have started patronizing these types of homes because they offer an appealing trade off that can be seen in the following advantages.

1. *Exceptional Value for Money*

These days, earning a decent living is hard enough. With plenty of restrictions to income for most people, finding cost-effective measures of daily living matters tremendously and this is one of the main reasons why there are individuals choosing to live in shipping container homes. Compared with other residential options in the market, it offers relatively cheap but desirable accommodations. Using shipping containers, it is possible to get hundreds of square feet of livable space at a fraction of the price of conventional homes. In the long run, the cost savings exceed rent savings as well. Not bad for owned property.

2. **Environmentally Friendly Component**

From solar panels to energy conserving LED lights, modern times have grown to embrace environmentally friendly products and services. Shipping container homes are in their own right eco-friendly housing options as there are thousands of these containers that are recycled into homes eliminating the need to manufacture additional building materials (cement, brick, mortar, wood for example) to satisfy the residential and commercial development demand. Recycling the steel instead of melting it down or scrapping also reduces the need for energy required for processing.

3. **Efficient Construction Timetable**

Because the initial structure already exists, fabricating a residence from shipping containers can be done in a short amount of time as compared with other types of homes. Having an efficient construction timetable means that homeowners get to enjoy their new house faster and have to incur fewer costs to do so. In construction, every day of work translates to significant expenses on labor. It is possible to prepare, build, wire, insulate, and decorate shipping container homes in a few weeks to a couple of months.

4. Viability of Off-Site Construction
Shipping container homes can be built on any parcel of land, even an enclosed garage, and can be transported to its final location later on. This viability for off-site construction is one of the many things that make this residential option extremely appealing. There are instances when certain areas are not conducive for building. It can be because of the limited space or the unavailability of constant sources of energy making the use of heavy-duty power tools hassling.

High-powered cranes are often used to deliver pre-fabricated shipping container shelters to their final location reducing the need for on-site prep or cleanup. (Image from www.containerhome.info)

Accessibility of Materials

As countries continue to engage in import and export trading, shipping containers will be readily available. Hundreds of thousands of these containers are used, reused, and repurposed making the concept of container homes easily justifiable not to mention highly sustainable.

5. Structural Strength and Durability

Shipping containers are very strong not to mention durable. Apart from being fabricated from steel, these were designed to stand constant exposure to the elements together with heavy loads and rough handling. They can stand up to earthquakes and other disasters thanks to their welded modular design. This is why they are excellent materials to use for home construction projects. These easily comply with ISO standards and have the ability to be stacked in multiple tiers. As they come equipped with built-in interlocking corner supports, fabricating multiple level homes using containers is safe not to mention easy to do. Those interested in a cost-effective and long-lasting residential solution will find shipping container homes truly beneficial.

6. Modular Design

Shipping containers carry a standard modular design. All containers carry the same width dimensions. In some cases, they differ by height and length but that is about it. There are two standard measurements for the latter so sourcing the right sized containers is still easy as pie. Aside from making residential design planning a breeze, it makes transport as simple as possible too. The modular design can also be attributed to the interlocking quality of these containers.

7. Transportability

Because of their primary purpose to transport products across continents, shipping containers have been built to satisfy transportation standards for shipment. Homeowners can easily have these transported via truck, rail, or ship, whichever works best.

8. **Minimal Labor Requirements**

Its modular design, interlocking component, and built-in support corners reduce the need for additional labor during the home construction process. Homeowners can easily cut costs on steel cutting and welding to name a few. When it comes to the design process, it only takes simple modifications to make the space adequate for living.

9. **Foundational Provision**

There is really no need to spend time on extensive foundational support as basic systems will work just fine. Shipping containers are designed in such a way that they have four support corners readily able to fit other containers and hold them in place. For as long as significant ground foundation is laid out, the structure will be good to go.

There are plenty of advantages that come with shipping containers used for residential purposes but it is also necessary for interested homeowners to consider the cons that come with this real estate trend.

Disadvantages of Shipping Container Homes

There are plenty of benefits that can be enjoyed by those who choose to live in a shipping container home but just like any other residential structure, it does come with certain disadvantages that one should be aware of as well.

1. Temperature Control

Shipping containers are made entirely out of steel and metals are known to be excellent conductors of heat. If used in areas where daily temperatures are at high levels, the experience will truly be a discomfort. It can be compared to living in an oven. When used in areas where temperatures tend to fall quite fast, the container can become extremely cold in an instant. Containers call for a little bit more than basic insulation to combat extreme weather conditions. In some cases, multiple layers of insulating materials including brick, wood, and padding may be required if the shipping containers will be utilized for residential purposes.

2. Humidity Control

Because the steel absorbs heat and cold fairly easily, temperature changes can easily cause moisture to over-develop. Given the isolated space, water beads can make the environment clammy. If left unattended to, rust will start to form. The problem with rust is that the minute it starts developing, it will continue to do so, slowly inching its way across the steel frame of the cargo unit.

Rusting shipping containers are not a new sight. Over time, the elements get the better of these units causing them to develop an amount of rust that can no longer be treated or remedied. (Image from www.flickr.com)

3. Flexibility Issues

One of the advantages of shipping containers is that they can be stacked together to allow for a larger living area. However, the problem with these cargo units is that although they can be stacked, builders are limited to containers of a default dimension. If these containers were to be opened at one side and connected horizontally, it will take an additional amount of time, effort, and expense.

4. Construction Requirements

Container homes can be constructed on or off site but there is a catch. Given the significant size of the units, they need to be transported using heavy machinery like forklifts and cranes. If the intended space where the home is to reside cannot accommodate the large equipment, there is no way for the container units to be transferred or delivered.

5. Building and Occupancy Permits

Building regulations depend on the area, zone, and purpose. There are certain rules that restrict the types of homes that can be built per location. Shipping container homes are not allowed in certain cities or neighborhoods so this can be a problem for the homeowner. Securing a permit for construction may be close to if not impossible. It would be best to consult with the local housing authorities on whether or not the idea is feasible for a particular area. Aside from container units per se, some places do not allow steel buildings to be built so this is another concern that has to be addressed.

6. **Floor Treatments**
Because of the nature of the material used in making shipping container homes, there are certain locational regulations that demand flooring to be treated with specialized insecticides prior to the installation of wooden flooring, tiles, or carpets. For shipping containers, the floors should be treated with a copper, chromium, and arsenic solution to kill off and prevent bacterial growth over time. If the floor area is not made of steel, any layering should be removed completely and disposed of prior to human habitation.

7. **Cargo Spillage**
Shipping containers are used to transfer various products across borders. In some cases, they carry non-perishable items but there are instances when they are used for perishable food products not to mention cargo that may be of a radioactive or dangerous nature like chemicals for example. Spillage cannot be prevented at all times so contaminants, some of which are undetectable, may leak onto the container. It a homeowner does not ensure proper cleansing prior to the build, this can lead to extreme and costly repercussions later on. Significant expense is necessary to clean a shipping container as abrasive cleansing is needed to be followed by sealant application.

8.   Manufacturing Solvents

Shipping containers are manufactured to cater to the purpose of storage or the transport of goods across countries. It is not designed to be lived in so most manufacturers make use of standard materials and solvents in the fabrication process. There are solvents used in painting or sealing the steel that can be harmful to humans even after they dry up. Again, to make a cargo unit suitable for living in, the steel should be stripped raw using abrasive materials and toner sealants.

9.   Structural Damage

Even the strongest materials are prone to wear and tear. As cargo shipping containers are used, they bear damage from friction not to mention collisions from improper handling. There are times when the force of heavy loads add to the damage as well. Some of the common damages seen in these units include twisted frames, pin holes, and cracked welds or seals. Although these can be repaired, it will cost a pretty penny to do so but if the damages are not addressed in time, rust may form causing even more problems for the builder planning on using them to build a home.

There are cases when the structural damage to the steel is of a grave degree. When this happens, it might be close to impossible to fix the walls making it better to simply trade in the steel for scrap.   (Image   from shippingcontainersforsale.com.au)

10. **Weak Areas**

The thing about steel shipping containers is that they are built to last. Because they are used for imports and exports and are exposed to harsh handling not to mention weather conditions, they are reinforced on all corners. But like all structures, these cargo units have their weak spots and one is on the roof. Standard shipping units can only accommodate a limit of about three hundred kilograms at a time. If a homeowner wants a multi-level shipping container home, this imposed but essential limit can easily reduce the potential of converting a space to meet specific living preferences.

Depending on the prospective shipping container homeowner, these cons might be enough to discourage them from making an investment into this housing type but it is a good thing to know how they can benefit from it and where problems may arise so that they can make an informed decision to move forward or scrap the idea completely.

Shipping Container Sustainability

These days, sustainability is a very important concept that many have embraced through the years. Resource conservation can come in the form of energy saving lights like LEDs or the use of recycled materials for varying purposes including construction. This is where intermodal shipping units enter the picture.

Although shipping container homes can be built using new containers, most homeowners choose to purchase used containers for their projects. By not having to manufacture additional steel cargo units for residential purposes, there is an immediate conservation of resources and energy. This means that aside from the reduction in carbon emissions during the build and use of shipping container homes, there can also be a reduction in embodied carbon emissions.

Shipping container homes can be connected to power grids but their transportability allows homeowners to live off the grid. The use of solar panel installations are quite popular in this type of residential endeavor. Aside from being able to save money on electricity and other utility expenses, homeowners can also live in an environmentally friendly fashion.

A number of people are unaware of the concept

of embodied carbon emissions. Over time, tons of reduction when it comes to this can result to years of conserved energy. Shipping container homes provide an alternative residential option that also opens doors to the conservation of everything from timber to the local landscape. It also helps protect water streams by controlling daily pollution. Traditional construction processes are responsible for a huge amount of the world's total air, noise, and water pollutants.

Permits and Legalities

Building a house from shipping containers does not make it less of a structure and this is why permits and licenses are still necessary. You might encounter contractors or building agents that will suggest forgoing permits to cut costs. Although offers like this are somewhat attractive, it is a trap that you should not fall for. If you do, you will be in violation of local ordinances. Not only can you be fined for it but you will miss out on vital inspections that will ensure that your structure is up to code; meaning that it is safe to live in. Without the necessary permits during the initial build, homeowners will also have a difficult time selling off the property when the time comes to do so.

Depending on the area, there may be various zoning and building regulations that apply to shipping container homes. Provided that everything has been taken care of, a homeowner can have a one-of-a-kind abode without much of the expense. (Image from www.inhabitat.com)

The process of securing permits together with local building code compliance are two of the most challenging hurdles that come with building shipping container houses. Because of its relatively new concept, and also due to the highly specialized niche market, there is currently no clear cut system in place. Standard building practices are applied when this type of infrastructure is constructed. Before an occupancy permit is granted by local housing agency officials, the homeowner must meet basic health and safety standards for the project. Building plans should be presented for approval and a final inspection is to be conducted after the build is completed.

When it comes to the building plans, it is possible for homeowners to draft these themselves for as long as they meet the requirements of the local housing agency. In some cases, the absence of an architect's stamp may fly but only for the initial draft. All plans for final approval must have the support and final outlay of a licensed architect lest they be rejected. The stamp ensures that a licensed professional has seen the plans and is taking responsibility for the integrity and design of the structure about to be built. If something were to happen, accidents for example, as a result of these plans, all liabilities will befall the architect. Shipping containers used for storage purposes no longer need this stamp but those to be used as homes do.

The need for permits may also stem from area classification. In most cases, permits are no longer needed in areas belonging to farm, ranch, or agricultural zones. Zoning is a matter that you need to pay attention to. Each zone has a distinct set of building and occupancy regulations that should be followed to a T. Making the mistake of missing out on satisfying even a single rule can lead to the building being deemed unfit for use. Aside from hefty fines and penalties, the structure could be torn down.

A good thing about zones is that they are pretty easy to check. Simply pay the local building department a visit and have your zone verified right then and there. Aside from checking zones and the regulations that they come with, you can also ask the same agency whether or not shipping container homes can be built in the area. They can also provide information on the specific permits needed for the construction if the zone allows for such infrastructures to stand. Be sure to note down who provided the information so that you have a name to mention should there be problems with regulations later on.

Especially if you will be obtaining the services of a general contractor, he or she can process all permits and licenses on your behalf. You do have the option of obtaining your own building permits as well but this will take time. You can even choose to build the structure yourself but only do so if you possess the same level of skills as the local contractors, builders, draftsmen, and architects in your area. If not, it would be logical not to mention cost-effective to let the professionals handle this task.

With shipping containers, the ones used to make homes are usually pre-owned. Unless they are sourced brand new, the homeowner must also obtain the necessary clearance from the health department deeming the container clean and safe enough to be converted into residential space. In some cases, these containers are used to ship perishable products commonly resulting in the development of bacterial residue. Used to transport other products, these can be left in cargo holding stations for months to years at a time leading to rust formation and the like. All of the shells have to be cleaned out via sand and water blasting and sealed for preservation before being used to construct a home.

Hiring a Contractor

It is always a wise decision to consult a reliable home contractor when it comes to a build like this. Choosing a reliable and trustworthy professional can make a huge difference when it comes to a job done properly or an utter nightmare. A rule of thumb is to steer clear from phone books and newspaper advertisements. Do not count on these things as the best professionals rarely require such marketing. These people get work through word of mouth from satisfied clients. Sourcing through referrals is the best option here as people have had a first-hand experience as to the kind of work a contractor can provide. They have seen him at work and can provide a certain level of expectation. Start by consulting family, friends, and neighbors that have had construction work done recently.

It is beneficial to have a reliable contractor because with the help of other professionals, he or she can transform a typical container unit into something truly out of the ordinary. (Image from shippingcontainersforsale.com.au)

Do not hesitate to ask. Here is an initial series of questions that you can ask the person who made the referral.

- Were you satisfied with the output?
- Was construction completed on time?
- Would you rehire this contractor?
- Were there issues with daily cleanup?
- Was the contractor approachable?
- Was the contractor open to sudden plan alterations?
- Did the contractor have his own team of workers?
- Did the contractor have his own materials suppliers?
- What was the agreed upon mode of payment and schedule?

Keep in mind that even if a contractor was referred to you, it is still necessary for you to run a complete background check and interview. It is a good idea to consider three to five potential applicants for your construction needs. Doing so provides you with options especially since these professionals may come to offer varying skills and services, not to mention fees. The most challenging aspect of any build, for a homeowner, is not the work itself but locating a competent contractor who can deliver quality output in a timely manner and reasonable costs.

When conducting your background check, work with local agencies, preferably those handling consumer affairs, or a chapter of the Better Business Bureau operating in your area. Check for blacklists, complaint histories, and the like. One or two offenses may be acceptable, within reason of course, but take repeated offenses as a red flag. Aside from checking a contractor's work history, check for licensing records as well. A contractor must pass a standard competency examination to be issued a license. The absence of this legal document also signals a red flag, possibly an illegal or limited practice. Keep in mind though that possessing a license does not equate with excellent workmanship. This is still something left for the client to decide. A license offers the sense of professionalism and commitment to the job at hand.

Insurance is essential. A contractor should be insured and the homeowner should have ample insurance coverage as well. Coverage for physical injuries on site, property damage, and natural disasters are necessary. See to it that a working comprehensive policy is in order before any of the work begins.

Significant effort is necessary but there are ways by which homeowners can spot questionable contractors. Here are red flags that you should be mindful of.
- Special or Bargain Prices

- High-Pressure Tactics or Overselling
- Refusal to Quote a Total Cost for the Build
- Failure to Provide Work References
- Unverifiable License Information
- Unverifiable Insurance Details
- Unverifiable Contact Information
- Non-existent Affiliation to Recognized Industry Associations
- Unsolicited Contact
- Leftover Material Accumulation

Oftentimes, a construction project requires several contractors --- a general contractor and subcontractors working under his or her command. The number of contractors needed for a build depends on the size of the project and the requirements imposed upon by the homeowner. A general contractor works by organizing the work schedule, securing the necessary permits, and coordinating with materials suppliers. The subcontractors serve to handle specific elements of the build. One may be hired to handle all of the electrical work and utilities while another may be in charge of built-in furnishings or external landscaping. In some cases, general contractors have teams of subcontractors that they can refer. If this network is unavailable, it will be the homeowner's responsibility to find these specialists one by one.

Searching for contractors is only one part of the equation. What follows is getting a bid from each prospect being considered. A written bid is necessary as it can be transformed into a binding contract. With any type of construction project, every correspondence has to be on paper. Be sure to get bids covering the same job tasks or output, manpower requirements, materials sourcing, and the like. This will make it easier for you to choose the best contractor to hire. Engaging in price negotiations during the bidding process is fine as long as all requests from both parties are reasonable. All bids and negotiations should be finalized before any contract is signed as altering parts of it later on can lead to more expenses on your part.

When the right contractor is chosen, a shipping container home or office is easy to attain. Here is an example of a great concept for a shipping container space. (Image from www.pinterest.com)

Just like any other product or service in the market, being cheap does not make it the best considerable option. In this line of work, price usually dictates quality. A home is something that is meant to last for a long time so paying a bit more for better output is worth doing. By paying more, a homeowner will not only be entitled to a better effort from the builders but better materials as well. Even if the costs are higher in the short run, the generated savings in the long run will be greater.

In negotiating a fair contract, make sure that the document spells out all the terms of the work involved as this will help both parties reduce or eliminate the occurrence of time-consuming and costly misunderstandings during the build. Here are the initial pieces of information that the contract should carry.

- Contractor's Name and Contact Information
- Contractor's License Information
- Subcontractors' Names and Contact Information
- Homeowners Name and Contact Information
- Agreed Upon Work Timetable (Start and Finish Dates Included)
- Agreed Upon Mode of Payment and Payment Schedule
- Scope of Work (Securing Permits Included)
- List of Materials Needed (Specifications Included)
- List of Machinery and Equipment Needed
- Demolition and Clean-Up Provisions

- Terms of the Agreement
- Arbitration Provisions (Dispute Clauses)
- Limitations of Liability for the Homeowner (Code Violations - Contractor Obligation)
- Insurance Provisions
- Signatures of Both Parties and the Date of Signing
- Addendum for Non-Inclusions to the Contract

Construction projects are normally done in phases and payments follow suit as they are settled in stages over the course of the build. This includes the delivery of key supplies and materials. A contractor will require a down payment of about ten percent or so. Protect yourself by not paying more than what is necessary during this stage. In most cases, even with initially trustworthy contractors, they have the tendency of using excess payments to finance projects of other clients oftentimes leaving the financier, you, high and dry as time passes.

Always be in communication with contractors. Aside from receiving frequent project updates, this enables all parties to resolve problems as early as possible. Resolving issues during the course of the build is better than having to attend to them after the turnover. Contractors, during the build, are keener on fixing problems like leaking roofs or faulty wiring and the like. Getting them to attend to these issues later on will be quite the challenge as they have already received payment for the initial service and won't be at a loss for the sloppy output. A good security measure to ensure that you are extended reasonable aftercare services is to include a clause in the contract allowing you to hold the final payment installment for a month after the turnover.

Aside from ensuring that all construction as per your specifications are met a hundred percent, the full payment to the main contractor should only be given after you have obtained signed documents covering payments to subcontractors, suppliers, and other expenses for the build. These official release papers are called mechanic's-lien waivers. They stand as receipts for services and products received. Without the formal release from obligation, these agencies can have a mechanic's lien placed against your house until all payables have been settled. Demand these waivers together with official receipts for all purchases and expenses from the general contractor.

Construction Process

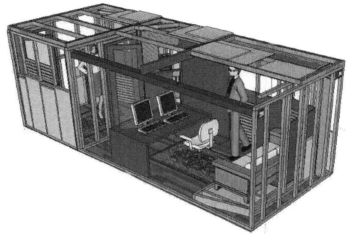

With some preparation, a modular shipping container can be programmed to serve the purpose of a livable residence. Careful floor planning will also allow homeowners to make most out of the available space offering them a different type but highly efficient kind of residence. (Image from www.renaissanceronin.wordpress.com)

Preparing Shipping Containers
Shipping containers can be bought new and if so they no longer need to be prepped before the build. If a homeowner has decided on purchasing used cargo units, it needs to pass several health and safety standards before it can be transformed into any living space may it be an office or an actual house. Part of the health and safety standards require that the units be

stripped raw and cleaned out prior to reuse.

When used for cargo, these containers may have been used to transport items that leak harmful chemicals and bacteria over time. Given enough time to culture, these can produce harmful vapors that oftentimes have no visible marks or scent making them dangerously undetectable. It is important that any dirt, dust, or debris are removed from the container. Abrasive materials, bristled brooms, and the like may be used for this process.

If a pressure washer is available then use it to greatly expedite the cleaning process. It would be best to get the help of a professional when it comes to any pressure washing as the process can overwhelm a non-expert. Start at the end of the container moving your way towards the main doors. Pay a lot of attention to the seams, the nooks, and all crannies you see. Check the floors for wear and tear as well. Excessive damage can raise a red flag.

Start cleaning the inside then move your way out of the container. If a pressure washer is used, it may be powerful enough to strip off any old paint not to mention rust that has formed on the steel. Any excess corrosion that cannot be initially removed can be treated with acidic compounds like vinegar. To hasten the process, rub the vinegar in using pieces of aluminum foil. Depending on the gravity of the rust situation, industrial cleaners may also be used. If the corrosion is excessive and have caused other, more serious, damages to the unit, it may be best to simply forego the particular container.

After it dries, do a secondary cleaning run by going over the container with some medium grit sandpaper on a belt or orbital sander. This serves the purpose of removing any remaining paint flakes. You do not have to strip off all of the old paint, just the areas which show signs of wear because if you don't, the new paint that you apply will peel off in no time. Prime the container to seal it against corrosion and any moisture. You can then apply any paint color of your choosing to the interior and exterior walls of the shipping container.

If the builder needs to cut portions out of any side walls, the cutting and sanding should be done prior to the priming and painting. This will save the builder a lot of time and money. When choosing paints, thicker solutions work best for steel shipping containers. Not only do they offer stronger and longer-lasting external seals but thick paints also stick better to the metal structures.

General Construction
Building any type of house, regardless of the size, is never a small feat. Aside from multiple materials and machinery, a number of tasks must also be accomplished by competent builders and design professionals. Part of the appeal of shipping container homes is the

simplification of the construction process that it offers. Before general construction begins, obtain all necessary permits and source materials from reliable suppliers. Also form a team of laborers depending on the magnitude of the task at hand. If a contractor is hired, he or she will be the one to handle these.

General construction begins with site work. This involves finding a designated location for the shipping container home. This is the time for groundwork. It may necessitate some excavation to lay the foundation in. At this time, plans for utilities, water management, and septic systems must also be laid out. The size of the main ground foundation depends on how many containers are included in the design plans and how much weight is expected to be held after construction is completed. The foundation should be strong enough to keep everything in place even when disasters like typhoons or earthquakes hit.

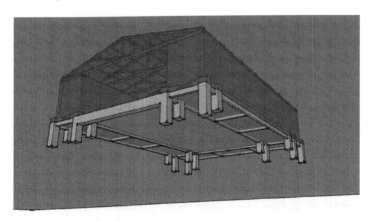

The foundation does not only serve to secure the shipping container house in place. It is also used to level the property where the containers will be positioned. (Image from www.pinterest.com)

The foundation can be built using precast concrete panels to make things easier for the builder. If a homeowner can afford the time, a stronger foundation can be created using hollow cement blocks and poured concrete. This goes atop an excavated area that can be filled with gravel to assist with drainage. As the foundation is laid out, builders can add insulating elements and water proofing components for a better final structure.

The process of setting the building's foundation is the trickiest step in the project because it must also address gas supply lines, utilities, and electrical wiring components. These are run from the base of the foundation to their respective positions in the home's floor plan. After all of these are taken care of, there is a matter of sealing the main foundation. Traditional methods make use of compacted soil, gravel, laid-out rebar, and more concrete on-pour.

Shipping containers have been designed to carry a modular outlay but these bodies can be modified to fit the needs of the homeowner. Although the corrugated steel walls have been fabricated to support heavy loads not to mention constant exposure to the elements, these can be cut to specifications with the proper equipment. In cases where modular units are placed side by side, not simply stacked atop one another, openings for internal entryways and windows can be cut into the units.

When it comes to these types of modifications, simple as they may seem, it would be best for professionals to be called in for assistance. Aside from an expert builder, a structural engineer, and an architect should also be contacted. This is because removing a portion of any wall or corner can significantly weaken the structure, reducing the weight that its roof can support. Aside from steel-cutting, welding and framing are other elements involved in the general construction of shipping container homes. Although these are important parts of the project, they can come at an expense and this is why modifications should only be done when extremely necessary.

After the foundation sets and the container units are prepared for final assembly, it is time to secure them to the foundation and each other. Each base unit is to be crane-lifted onto the foundation, hooked, and welded down. Because of the weight of these container units, it does not take much to secure them into place. Corner fasteners are all that is necessary to hold them onto the foundation. Additional support can be installed through the use of corner concrete blocks. Containers can then be secured to one another, vertically or horizontally, by making welds. If several units are to be stacked atop one another, additional support beams as dictated by the structural engineer should be utilized.

Internal and external entryways, windows, and other openings should then be framed. The most common method used by builders for shipping container homes begins with steel frames, which are then reinforced by wooden ones. Because of the limited amount of living space provided by cargo units, sliding doors and windows are commonly used. In this case, the steel and wood double frames can be made to run on wheels through L-section panels.

The house is now ready for insulation to be installed. Utility systems and electrical wiring are also run through the home at this point. When the walls have been sealed and all finishes completed, interior plans from painting to furniture arrangements to the installation of fixtures are then satisfied. Depending on the location, external landscaping may be necessary to add to the home's aesthetic value. Everything then goes under inspection before a certificate of occupancy can be attained.

Given the often miniscule size of shipping container homes, as compared to its traditional residential structural counterparts, this process will take about several weeks to several months to complete. The steps are fairly similar to constructing a traditional house but faster to complete. Homeowners that have adequate skills in building can tackle a project like this themselves but for most, the best route is to go with professional laborers.

Insulation

The insulation does not only act as a temperature control component but a secondary barrier that protects the internal part of the shipping container home. (Image from www.greenmyhomenow.com)

A very important part of the construction process for shipping container homes is insulation. Given the type of structure builders will be working with, it is necessary for above standard insulation methods to be applied. The need for insulation depends on where the container home will be placed. Locations where temperatures can rise or fall with ease demand insulation. Insulation is an important component to any house build. It can come at quite at expense but will save the homeowner from intense temperatures not to mention prevent or reduce the home's susceptibility to condensation which is responsible for rust and mold formation.

Given that the home requires insulation, the next question to ask pertains to how much insulation is necessary and what type of material will work best to satisfy this measure. Colder climates call for more insulation to keep a shipping container home warm. Insulation in this case serves the secondary purpose of controlling condensation. Usually, cold environments are prone to excessive rainfall. When deciding over insulating materials, this is another aspect that has to be considered. Aside from keeping the steel structure warm, creating a seamless barrier against rain is also necessary.

In areas with a warmer climate, insulation may be necessary but not in the same amount. Here, insulation is needed to prevent as much heat as possible from being absorbed by the steel structure. The goal now is to keep the internal temperature of the home at a relatively low and comfortable, livable level. There are four main categories that apply when it comes to home insulation. These serve varying purposes and are intended on providing different levels of insulation to a structure. It would be best to consult a contractor to know which type works best given the conditions mentioned above.

1. **Eco-Friendly Insulation**

Environmentally friendly alternatives to traditionally manufactured insulation products are readily available these days and offer the same service without leaving a massive carbon footprint. Here are some examples of commonly used insulation materials and methods that are greener in nature.

● Living Roof Systems

A living roof is not exactly a roof that is alive. It is not a direct form of insulation as well. What it is, is a design element that helps the homeowner control temperatures within the home. It is a moving, convertible roof that can be repositioned during the summer months and reverted back when the rainy season kicks in. It is best described as a sloped roof.

During the summer months, the hot air that builds up in the home is allowed to escape. Any cool air is then allowed into the container as it gets pushed in through the roof. It follows the concept of hot air rising and cold air sinking. This can be used together with basic home insulation to give the homeowner better control over temperatures in a shipping container abode.

● Cotton Insulation

Cotton insulation is another spin-off of the

blanket type insulation product. In this case, what replaces the fiberglass or rock wool is a bunch of recycled clothing. Just like sheep's wool, cotton is a naturally-occurring product. It is a renewable resource that can be grown in a short span of time making it an ideal component for such an in-demand product. Unlike sheep's wool though, cotton is fairly expensive so unless a builder plans on using old clothes in the process, the synthetic option may be better.

- Mud Insulation

The past years saw the rise of mud as an excellent material that can be used to build homes on its own. For those who do not plan on living in a mud house, the same material can be used for insulation instead. It is best applied to shipping container homes meant to be positioned in locations where the climate is not only hot but dry as well. It has the capacity to keep heat out and retain a cool internal temperature.

Although not as aesthetically attractive as other available options, mud insulation works extremely well in keeping the heat out and promoting a cool inner environment. (Image from kareaconstructionenglish.wordpress.com)

For typical homes, the mud is simply padded onto the walls and allowed to dry and set. In the case of shipping container homes, the mud can be cladded onto the external walls and roofing. Since the container is made out of steel, the builder will have to use battens as these will keep the mud in place. Battens refer to a solid strip of material usually fabricated from plastic, metal, or fiberglass. Mud insulation is not ideal for areas where there is frequent rainfall as excess moisture is its weakness.

1. **Wool Insulation**

Most comparable to blanket insulation is the eco-friendly wool variety. It follows a relatively similar concept. The only difference is that instead of fiberglass or rock wool, sheep's wool is used to create the blanket. It reduces one's carbon footprint because it reduces the need to manufacture the synthetic materials. It utilizes natural sheep's wool making it a sustainable and naturally occurring product.

2. Foam Insulation

One of the best but costly types of insulation is that of the spray foam variety. It is expensive because it is extremely simple to apply. You just spray it to the desired spot from a can and you are good to go. As it leaves the vacuum of the spray can, the closed-cell polyurethane foam expands and hardens taking the shape of wherever it was sprayed on. This means that it can get into the tightest nooks and crannies of a structure creating a seamless barrier as it hardens into place. As no space is left uncovered, no air pockets or gaps are left. Air pockets are the primary origin of corrosion and mold-causing moisture and bacteria.

Aside from being the easiest to use, it is readily available and provides the highest rating based on industry standards. The rating quality given to insulating materials are based on qualities including their ability to resist heat flow. The better a particular material is at resisting heat, the higher the rating it garners. If there is a downside to this form of insulation, it may be that it is messier to use compared to its counterparts.

The beauty of spray foam is that it is the type of insulation that can be applied to both the internal and external walls of shipping containers used to make livable homes. It can also be sprayed underneath the structure to stop ground moisture from penetrating the steel container. As it sets, the builder can choose not to cover it with anything else and move onward to the painting, sealing, and finishing. Before it dries, it can be smoothened to look like fine concrete when it hardens.

3. **Blanket Insulation**

Roll, also referred to as blanket, insulation is commonplace in the construction industry. It is the cheapest of all available insulation materials in the market. Just like panel insulation, it calls for stud walls and can only be placed within these confines. These normally come fabricated from rock wool, which is a mineral compound or fiberglass.

It is pretty easy to use although some people have encountered problems fitting the material into wall gaps. Especially when the fiberglass variety of this material is chosen, it requires special handling. Protective equipment like gloves, safety glasses, and masks are needed for the builder to safely install these into the walls.

Yes, it makes for a cost-saving measure but with the amount of effort required to install it, other alternatives might be better considered.

4. **Insulation Panels**

Common and extremely user-friendly for DIY-ers is the panel insulation variety. Panels can be bought at hardware and construction depots and can be bought in various sizes or dimensions. There are predefined sizes available for sale or builders can have these specially cut to size to suit their design plans. The builder must have stud walls to fit these in. They are to be positioned in between the gaps in the wall. Compared to blanket insulation, these are easier to fit into walls but are more costly as a result.

Given its small depth, this type of insulation bears a high insulation ranking making them an excellent and more cost-effective alternative to foam insulation. Its high ranking also allows homebuilders to keep the insulation thickness to a minimum while attaining the same level of temperature control for the shipping container. Aesthetically, these can only go in between walls, not on exposed parts of the structure.

The type of insulation that best applies to any shipping container home depends on the climate of the chosen location, the homeowner's budget, and of course, the structure's capacity for modification. All of these elements should be taken into account before any particular option is chosen as it can be quite costly to change plans later on during the build.

Insulation panels come in different widths and can be cut according to the builder's specifications. They are usually made out of a hardened foam composite. (Image from www.varmefhs.co.uk)

Costing

With the housing market in a vulnerable stage and with a majority of people having difficulties affording rent, there is always the continuous hunt for cheaper, more affordable forms of housing. The concept of tiny house living has grown tremendously popular through the years and it has given rise to alternative forms of housing including shipping container homes. But shipping container houses have grown larger in the past years with some measuring as large as traditional homes without as much of the cost.

Shipping container homes, or the steel cargo units used in making them, primarily originate from China and other parts of Asia. They are actually considered to be some of the most popular exports received by countries across the globe. These cargo units allow for the safe and secure delivery of different products across oceans and also serve the purpose of standing as building blocks for unique and environmentally friendly homes. These days, a huge number of international freight are delivered in steel containers that can be stacked upon each other and stored on ship decks, offloaded onto tractor trailer backs, and carted into trains. In some cases, these cargo containers are shipped back to the source for reuse. Other times, they are stored empty in shipment container graveyards.

There are ways to recycle these containers if they are no longer meant to be reused. It is possible to scrap the steel or melt it down or the containers can be cleaned out and used as building blocks for shipping container homes. The latter promotes the lowest carbon footprint making it a viable solution to the need and demand for ample housing around the world. Thanks to the influence of architects, these units have not only been converted into storage houses but residential homes, guest houses, studios, offices, retail store spaces, and many more. Container units come prefabricated with a couple of standard sizes. To make them suitable for residential living, architects have found a way to modify them increasing the amount of livable space that homeowners interested in shipping container homes can enjoy. When positioned side by side, these can provide thousands of square footage, which can further be increased by having containers stacked atop one another.

The cost of this kind of home depends primarily on how many shipping containers will be used during construction. It starts with the type of shipping container to be used. These can be bought new or used. New ones definitely cost more while used container units can be bought for several thousand dollars to three thousand dollars on average. What homeowners get for this amount is a complete structure readily available for modification. Made out of solid steel and welded together in the best possible way, these structures are extremely durable and offer an excellent yet cost-effective base or foundation for a house meant to be lived in for years on end. An architect by the name of Adam Kalkin was able to construct a 2000 square foot home from six shipping containers. The total cost of the shipping container house from the cargo units to the modifications, insulation, finishes, furnishings, and other design elements only amounts to $120000, which is pretty cheap compared to traditional houses in the market.

A shipping container home made from three modular units modified to co-exist as a single living space. (Image from homeinabox.blogspot.com)

The only catch with shipping container homes is that more often than not it is the homeowner who must own the land that it resides in. Aside from purchasing the container units and spending on the land, homeowners must also shoulder various costs which include the securing of permits, utilities connections, electricity grid connections, and gas connections to name a few. Depending on the homeowner, he or she can reduce the carbon footprint even more by installing solar panels in the home. A basic solar setup would cost about five thousand dollars depending on how green a homeowner wants to go. There are people who live completely off the grid and have a complex solar panel setup in their shipping container home. Although it may come at a large initial expense, it generates an excess of savings over time. With this type of home, it can be built in a relatively short period. This means that labor expenses usually measure to about a third of what a traditional house may cost to build or renovate.

For those who want to live in a shipping container home, provided that they have the land to house it in and their area permits this type of residence, here are the initial sources of expense that come with such a project.

- Steel Containers
- Site preparation (foundation)
- Assembly and modification of cargo units
- Installation of insulation, heating, and cooling systems
- Plumbing
- Electricity
- Roofing
- Flooring
- Furnishings
- Windows and entryways

- External landscaping
- Other finishing

The thing about shipping container homes is that they can be built off-site and delivered to the final location ready to be lived in. If this is the option chosen by the homeowner, he or she should add the corresponding shipping costs to the total expense. Depending on how far the delivery point is, this can amount to several thousand dollars of additional expense.

The $120000 spent by architect Kalkin resulted to an extravagant shipping container home but an amount as little as $20000 can provide an ample shelter complete with a front porch. This amount can easily yield a 350 square foot home that is perfect for a bachelor's pad. For this type of home, construction will usually take several weeks to a couple of months.

Before investing in this type of house, it is good to plan everything from assuring the availability of land, securing permits, checking local zoning and building regulations, and setting aside a reasonable budget for the build. Usually, overall costs go beyond what was originally quoted. So as not to be overwhelmed by any additional expense, it would be wise to set aside an additional ten to twenty percent of the total budget for emergency needs.

Planning Your Home

When it comes to a shipping container home, if homeowners will be sticking to a standard structure with minimal modifications and a limited amount of space, then they should plan their home design accordingly. There are plenty of excellent sources for space-saving floor plans that will allow homeowners to have several fully functional areas in a modular unit.

Here is a sample floor plan that can be applied to a shipping container home. The amount of space allotted per functional area depends on what the homeowner needs. With some careful plotting, simple modular containers can be transformed into one-of-a-kind living areas. (Image from www.odpod.com.au)

Depending on the available square footage,

homeowners should focus on four main areas. These are the bedroom, bathroom, kitchen, and living areas. Generally, the living area should have the largest space allotment out of the four, as it will be the place where the most amount of time will be spent. It would be best to combine the kitchen and living area into a free flowing space that will also serve the purpose of acting as a convertible dining area.

The bedroom can exist without a separate wall or door. In this case, it is a great idea to use simple wall dividers that can provide the necessary privacy offering without taking up too much room in the modular unit. Wall dividers can easily be positioned to increase or decrease the amount of available space in each area. If there is a room that needs the utmost privacy, it will be the bathroom. It would be best to secure this with a lockable door but go with sliding ones instead of traditional swivels.

When planning a shipping container home, everything should be decided according to the specific needs of the homeowner. A good move would be to work closely with an architect and interior designer who can provide the best insight as to how a space can be arranged to deliver an outcome that will be up to par.

Floor Plans and Building Ideas for Your Home

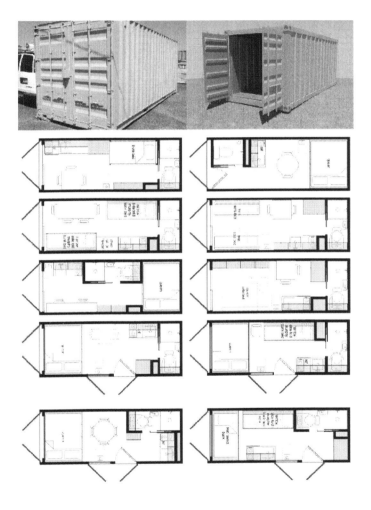

Here are some sample floor plans that can be considered by those who are new to the entire shipping container home concept. These plans are for single modular units and as can be seen offer the best use of space for every available square foot. (Image from www.tinyhouseliving.com)

When it comes to floor plans and design blueprints, homeowners will require the assistance of competent professionals. An architect, a structural engineer, and an interior designer can help determine the best placements for furnishings and divisions for rooms not to mention identify where extra supports may be necessary. Landscapers can provide assistance on the outside part of the home.

The Internet is an excellent place to start looking for ideas prior to the build. There are tons of free resources that can be accessed with the click of a button. Some, more professional, layouts may be obtained for a minimal fee. The beauty of the Internet is that aside from offering a wide variety of options to interested homeowners, it is also a great resource where people can find feedback on these designs; how they work, what can be changed, what is advisable versus what is not, and so on and so forth.

Together with the assistance of professionals, it is extremely important for homeowners to at least have some idea of what they want their home to look like and carry. It will surely make the design process easier and faster for everyone and it will allow for the least amount of expense. With everything identified beforehand, costly mistakes can be avoided.

Working with Small Spaces and Limited Weight Capacities

Depending on how many shipping containers homeowners plan to utilize in their construction, the amount of livable space may be quite limited in certain cases. Because of how shipping container homes are unlike traditional houses in different ways, it is important for potential homeowners to be fully aware of the restrictions that may come with this choice of residence. Not only will there be a more limited amount of space to work with but when container units are stacked, there is also a weight limit for the upper tiers.

To live comfortably despite the lesser or fixed space allotment, homeowners should be mindful not only of their choice of furniture but everything that they bring into the home. If multiple shipping container units will be stacked atop one another, the assistance of a structural engineer should be attained. The structural engineer will be the one to assess the allowable weight limit for the tiers. In some cases, additional support beams or posts may be installed in the bottom tier to make the upper units as functional and safe as possible.

Since shipping container units come in fixed dimensions, a great way to have access to more space, for as long as the homeowner's budget permits, is to put several containers side by side. With the help of a professional contractor, entryways can be cut into the units and reinforced. With proper planning, the space restrictions of shipping container homes can easily be counteracted offering homeowners the possibility of a non-traditional, cost-effective, and highly efficient abode that will last for decades.

Shipping containers can be stacked but may require additional support beams for safe residential usage. (Image from www.jetsongreen.com)

Organization and Design Hacks for Your Home

As what was previously mentioned, a standard shipping container home can provide enough space but one in limited quantities. In this case, it would be best for the homeowner to adapt to a minimalist lifestyle or improve on his or her organizational skills around the house. Aside from choosing to apply multiple functionalities per area of the house, simple practices of organizing things around the home can do a lot of good. Here are some organizational and design hacks that will be well worth the knowledge. Not only will they allow for a cleaner looking space but over time, they will help homeowners focus more on what they need instead of what they simply want.

Bedroom

The bedroom is one of the most if not the most important part of any home as it offers a place for rest, relaxation, and refuge. This is why it should be kept organized at all times. Although clutter does foster creativity, it keeps the mind awake and alert. At the time when a person only wants nothing but to rest, this is not the best thing in the world, for the brain to remain active when it should not be. Especially in a standard shipping container home where space allotment is quite limited, using the right furnishings and keeping personal belongings intact is highly necessary.

Adapting to a minimalist lifestyle may be a challenge at first but it can be extremely rewarding later on. The thing about minimalism is not restricting ownership but focusing on the important things, what is essential around the house, what has function, need versus want. Not only will it help you with organization but it will also help you save money for other, more necessary, purposes.

In the bedroom, the essential pieces of furniture include the bed, a closet, and a bedside table. These days, there are plenty of available sources for multi-functional furniture. This can mean having storage underneath the bedframe, a nightstand that can function as transformable seating, and a closet that can have a built-in dresser.

When it comes to the bedroom, it is important to keep things orderly. The minute a fresh batch of laundry comes in, immediately put the items in the closet. Do not leave the task for later. More often than not, you will tend to push it further until your clothes are left in a corner. Be mindful of floor space. Always keep in mind that if it can be stored, keep it out of sight, and if it can be hung, keep it off of the floors. A number of excellent lighting and ventilation fixtures can be screwed onto the walls giving a stylized effect while helping maintain the vision of a large floor area.

To further maximize the space and keep the bedroom serene, be selective when it comes to the choice of color. Go with light pastels or calming earth tones like tans and greys. Accent it with white or cream moulding for an elegant overall look. Keep the window treatments as simple as you can but never ignore function. These should be thick enough to keep most of the light out but not too thick that they make the space look smaller than it actually is.

Everything that is not supposed to be part of the bedroom should be kept elsewhere. If there is a room in the shipping container house that needs the most effort, it is this. Make sure that it is a place for rest and nothing else.

Living Area

The living area will surely be the busiest part of the house. It will also be the primary area where homeowners will be entertaining visitors and guests over time. This is the reason why, even with a limited amount of space, ample seating may be required. It is a good thing that there are plenty of furniture offerings these days that allow for multiple functionalities.

A compact living room setup in a traditional single unit intermodal shipping container home. (Image from www.domain.com.au)

The living area is where the entertainment section should be. For a typical modern day homeowner, this may include a television set and its accompanying sound system and video playback equipment. Depending on the homeowner type, video game consoles might also be a part of the equation. Flat screen television sets are all the rage these days and in a shipping container home, these are ideal because they carry a sleek design and can easily be hung from the wall.

Traditionally, sound system speakers, game, and video consoles are kept in an entertainment cabinet. If you can find one that does not occupy that much space, this is one of the easiest organizational options available today. Having a lax budget means you can even have one built for your house suiting your specifications to a T. To make the process simpler, vie for hanging shelves instead. These are strong, durable, and can be hung in any way the homeowner pleases.

Again, by taking advantage of and maximizing the available vertical space, you can keep things off the floors and maximize the visible horizontal area in your shipping container home. If the wall structure permits, all wiring can be drawn through the walls into a common exit point lessening the look of clutter from multiple cords.

Then comes seating. A comfortable sofa is important. Since the area will be the busiest one in the home, there should be no question when it comes to the need to invest in good furniture. If you are the type of homeowner who frequently has guests over, it will be a good idea to purchase a convertible sofa bed. It can work well as seating during the day but also allow you to provide a cozy bed for people staying overnight. The best part is that the bed can conveniently be tucked back into place after usage. No muss, no fuss.

Additional seating and storage can be provided by box ottomans. These can also double as end tables for the living room. Simply position a piece of glass or wood atop it and you have yourself a makeshift coffee table centerpiece. When it comes to lighting fixtures, again, suspended varieties work best.

Kitchen

In a shipping container home, it is important for sufficient ventilation to be applied to the kitchen area especially if homeowners are active cooks. With the help of a structural engineer, several windows can be cut from the steel cargo unit and replaced with efficient exhaust systems. This is a very important initial step that should never be ignored.

When the ventilation has been taken care of, homeowners should then address the function of the kitchen. Will it be used solely for cooking and food preparation or will it double as a breakfast nook if not a dining area as well? If the space will only be used as a designated kitchen for cooking then homeowners should invest in the appliances that they need.

Most home kitchens come equipped with a stovetop, an oven, an overhead exhaust, a microwave, a toaster, and a coffee maker. Sounds like much but these are the basic appliances that go into a typical kitchen. If the allotted space and budget allows for all of these to be purchased then by all means purchase them. If the homeowner wants to keep the space simple but still have that food prep function then the toaster, coffee maker, and microwave may be scrapped from the list. It is fairly easy to heat meals, boil water for coffee, and toast bread on the stove top.

Here is an industrial-inspired kitchen in a shipping container home. Notice that it has all of the important components that a kitchen needs yet is arranged in such a way that gives the perspective of a wide and open space. (Image from www.containerhome.info)

The necessity of the stovetop and oven is self-explanatory. As for the overhead exhaust, in addition to the kitchen windows and general exhaust system, it will easily help homeowners control food smells that can penetrate walls and furniture. It also works tremendously well in controlling the excess heat that may circulate around the kitchen and the shipping container home. As it is positioned directly above the stovetop, it can immediately absorb the emitted heat and food smells while the homeowner cooks.

If the kitchen will double as a dining area, sufficient dining and seating provisions should be considered. This means that homeowners should invest in a table for starters. If there is a limited amount of space to work with, a kitchen island can work well as a preparation area and dining table in the kitchen. A makeshift bar can also be considered in this case. It can easily double as a room partition and the homeowner can take advantage of its multi-functionality. The number of chairs depends on how many people live in the home. Usually, four seats are the standard. If there is enough space to work with, this can be extended to eight followed by a round table that can be used to entertain guests. If the available space is limited, two to four chairs will work just fine. Provided that there are multi-function furniture in other areas of the house, like the living room perhaps, these can then be used for extra seating when needed.

Next comes the pots and pans. A home cook will surely love to have an assortment of pots and pans in different colors but an excess of these items can lead to clutter not to mention unnecessary spending. Instead of purchasing a number of these, consider investing in three to five kinds but those of excellent quality. Not only will they last longer but they will take up less space in the kitchen as well. Keep in mind that these will be used one to a couple at a time so there really is no need to have tons of them lying around the house.

The same goes for plates, glasses, mugs, utensils, and cutlery. Only purchase what is necessary.

Have an extra set just in case but nothing more. If there will be a party at the house, consider getting their disposable counterparts. Not only are these affordable but cleanup will also be a breeze. Just chuck them in the trash after use and you are good to go. No muss, no fuss, no mess, no hassle.

Do not forget about the pantry. Every kitchen must have a pantry to store various ingredients and ready-to-eat food items in. The pantry environment should be dry and cool as to keep food fresher for a longer period. Do what it takes to prevent pests from getting at the food. There are different products that can readily be bought at hardware stores for this purpose.

In a shipping container home, a pantry can be built into the structure much like a bedroom closet. When homeowners go for the built-in storage, they can easily maximize the vertical space allotment in their homes. Further increase the amount of available storage by having retractable shelving installed in the main pantry cabinet. These will make for more storage that can be accessed with ease. Just a quick pull will give homeowners access to the ingredients that they need for the meal they are preparing.

Label everything. Stick-on labelers are readily available today and it can be used to organize spices and other ingredients inside the pantry. Another part of pantry organization is checking and monitoring all product packages and labels for expiration dates. There is no sense in keeping food in store when it can no longer be consumed. This is only a waste of space not to mention a potential hazard should there be kids in the house. They might end up ingesting something that has already passed its safe consumption period. A quick check every couple of weeks will be enough to ensure that the pantry is always in tiptop shape and that everything it contains is safe for everyone in the family.

Just like the other parts of the home, be sure to have a place for everything. A drawer for cutlery, cupboards for plates and the like, storage walls for pots and pans, and so on and so forth. An organized kitchen will not only allow for a cleaner space but one that is easy to work in as well.

Bathroom

A shipping container home can provide ample space for a bathroom. Utilizing the streamlined approach will make it appear bigger than it actually is. Here is an example of a bathroom used in a single container home. (Image from www.co-tain.com)

Now comes the bathroom. The rule of thumbs for bathrooms is that they should be kept as simple as possible but able to satisfy all of the homeowners needs. There are only four components necessary to make a bathroom complete. Here they are.

- Sink
- Toilet
- Shower Area
- Storage for Towels and Toiletries

For most people, the sink is the first thing they use when they enter the bathroom upon waking up. They wash their face, brush and floss their teeth, and proceed with their daily regimen from there. There is really no need to spend a lot of money on a sink because it provides a fairly basic function. The important component that homeowners should pay attention to is the faucet. This fixture is important as it controls the amount of water being pumped onto the sink. A long-headed curved faucet works best by offering a substantial amount of space between the water source and the sink. This extra space makes it easier for homeowners to wash their face, collect water, and the like. It allows for less water wastage too. For the knobs, go with traditional spin knobs instead of the variety that runs on sensors.

The toilet. Unlike the sink, it will be a wise decision to spend a bit more on the toilet fixture. These need to be durable enough to handle the daily wear and tear and should be large enough to offer a comfortable experience to those using it. Aside from the size and quality of the toilet, homeowners should also invest money in the flushing system. These days, there are multiple mode systems that help conserve water. These come with two to three buttons. Each button is designated to release a certain amount of water when pressed so homeowners do not have to resort to a full flush, one that empties the entire water reservoir, every single time.

These days, there is a new product that aims to help homeowners save even more water in their bathrooms. It is a combined sink and toilet setup. The way it works is that the faucet is linked to the main water line while the sink is connected to the toilet water reservoir. Homeowners get a gush of clean water from the faucet which they can use as they please. The used water then flows down the drain of the sink into a pipe that is connected to the toilet water reservoir filling it with used water. There is no need to waste clean water to flush the toilet. As the reservoir fills up, this used water can then be recycled as flushing water.

And then comes the shower. Homeowners that have ample space and a higher working budget can equip their shipping container home with a bathtub and shower setup. For those who only have the option of choosing one of these normally go for the traditional shower. This part of the bathroom is pretty simple to address. All that is needed is enough space for a person to move in. It would be best to apply tiles to the designated area from the floor to about a half of the wall. This allows for easy maintenance. The tile also protects the outer wall from excess water exposure. To control water flow, have a half-foot barrier built on the floor separating the shower area from the rest of the bathroom. Use either a shower curtain or a glass partition to complete the look.

Just like the sink area, it is the shower fixture that needs more attention here for the same purpose of controlling water flow. A simple shower can be made more luxurious with the help of a multi-function shower head. This type of shower head offers several water release features some of which even provide a massaging effect. These are not that expensive and can be bought from any hardware store. Again, twist knobs always work best and when it comes to water heaters, go with the variety that can be installed inside the structural wall. It is safer to use as electrical wires are protected from water exposure.

Finally, a complementary feature to any bathroom at home is the storage cabinet for towels and toiletries. A common practice is having a shelf or two installed underneath the sink again utilizing the available vertical space to save on the horizontal one. If there is ample ceiling space, homeowners can also choose to have a cabinet built from the ceiling down to about a third of the total wall. The cabinet is meant for towels, paper napkins, toiletries, and all other products needed for a bathroom and nothing else.

Bathrooms are pretty easy to clean so this should not be a bother. Once every week, run some hot water from the shower with the bathroom door closed to create steam. A few minutes will do the trick. This steam is all it takes to clean all fixtures and remove any bacteria that might have settled into any nooks and crannies. A complete wash down with soap and water every month will also ensure that the bathroom is gleaming clean. Be sure to wipe everything down dry.

Some additional elements that you can install in a bathroom include a towel hanger and of course, a mirror by the sink. Try to avoid old school medicine cabinets and choose a thin mirror instead. Forego any special finishing and just have the edges sanded down and sealed to ensure that the glass does not cut anyone by accident. Have this screwed onto the wall and that is about it. To control any unpleasant odors, a simple bowl of potpourri will be enough. Place this by the toilet reservoir. Potpourri usually expels all of its scent after thirty days. By then, get some essential oils and mix several drops with about a third of a glass of water. Spray the solution onto the potpourri and let everything dry completely

Home Office

A home office has a specific function just like other areas of the house. There are homeowners who have this in their houses while others simply add a working desk to their living area for such a purpose. If a homeowner has the space and budget for a designated home office, it can be designed in such a way that all of the things necessary to have a functional office is made available but arranged neatly allowing for a compact space.

A good working desk is important in any home

office. This should be large enough to fit a laptop, pens, notepads, and the like. If possible, go for a desk that has drawers underneath. Not only will these allow for more storage but these will help keep items intact and organized. For most people, a significant amount of time is spent in a home office. This is why a good and comfortable chair is also worth the investment. An ergonomic chair should be considered as it offers excellent support for the back.

A home office can be as simple or as grand of a space depending on what the homeowner prefers. (Image from www.homedit.com)

Invest in a good computer as well. Desktop computers are still popular but for a compact home office, portable gadgets work best. In this case, investing in a quality laptop computer is a better direction to take. The great thing about a laptop computer, aside from being able to fit inside a desk drawer, is that it can be taken to and from the shipping container home without much of a hassle. It allows for remote work to be possible whenever necessary. It may come with a slightly higher expense at first but this cost can easily be outweighed through proper care and usage.

Often taken for granted, a dedicated desktop lamp is also essential when it comes to any home office setup. Even if the room already houses lighting fixtures, there are times when these are not enough to provide the necessary lighting for a desk. There are small table lamps that can readily be bought these days and they are not that expensive making them an excellent addition to any home office.

Complete the home office with a fax machine and printer. There are available machines these days that offer both services through a single piece of equipment and modern designs are compact enough not to be a bother. Although most transactions these days are done paperless, there are some documents that need to be printed out every now and then. There are a number of businesses that continue to rely on faxing rather than simply using emails and online document transfers. For printers, concentrate on models that use toner cartridges instead of standard printer ink. The former is more cost-effective and less prone to fading over time. Get a printer that can accommodate different paper sizes as well.

Make sure everything has its place and that everything is readily available not to mention within reach to make your home office an efficient area of your shipping container home.

Outside the Home

For the outside part of the home, basic landscaping can do a lot of good. Removing weeds, trimming the hedges, and watering the external part of the home is all it takes to maintain it, keeping it as clean as possible and preventing pests and similar nuisances. The external part of the shipping container home does not require as much maintenance as the inside but it should not be taken for granted. It significantly improves the aesthetic quality of the home and structure-wise, maintaining the outer walls prevents any unforeseen issues from happening like the development of rust or structural imbalance, foundational problems, and so on and so forth.

Maintaining the yard is quite simple. Maintaining the structure itself requires a bit more effort. To keep the outer walls of the shipping container clean, weekly hosing is all it takes. To prevent the onset of unwanted rust, be sure to let it dry completely after washing. If necessary, grab a cloth to dab out any excess moisture especially from the nooks and crannies of the container unit. A semi-annual touch up of primer, paint, and sealant will help maintain the container's aesthetic value while protecting it from the wear and tear of the elements.

As for the foundation, have it inspected at least once a year. In some cases, it might require patching or reinforcing. A contractor can help homeowners sort things out. Especially in areas where there is excessive rainfall or extreme heat, the foundation should not go unaddressed. It is always better to take care of issues while they are young and require minimal repair than have to worry about them when they are already full-blown as this will incur more costs not to mention more stress for the homeowner.

Simple Tips for Clutter Control

For some, controlling clutter may be a daunting task. In reality, although it can be quite challenging at first, especially if it is not second nature to a homeowner, it grows easier over time. It revolves around establishing a habit of cleaning and organizing that when done regularly becomes less of a chore and more of a daily involuntary routine.

The first rule to clutter control is keeping things in their proper place. Everything should have a home. For example, clothes go into the closet, pots and pans stay in the kitchen, and so on and so forth. Most of the time, forgetting to keep things in their place is what gives rise to clutter and as it grows in volume, homeowners become less keen on trying to organize every single thing. It is the overwhelming feeling of having plenty of things to organize that can be attributed to this flailing desire to clean up.

Next is to focus on what is necessary and only what is necessary. Although this does not mean depriving yourself of the things you want for your home, it encourages homeowners to shift their attention to what a home needs, what has function. It is okay to buy accents every now and then but these should be kept to a minimum. Even if they add elegance or pizzazz to a space, they can also become dust bunnies and later on, sources of clutter, when left to go out of hand.

It is also important for homeowners to apply a regular cleaning schedule. For a shipping container home, weekly cleaning should be done to keep things orderly and hygienic while monthly general cleaning is necessary to keep everything in tip top shape. Monthly cleaning includes total home maintenance, which means that fixtures, wiring, insulation, and other important aspects of the house should be checked for repairs and the like. In some cases, professional help may be necessary and if so, it would be wise to spend on it than regret scrimping later on.

Every year, conduct a cleanup of the entire home. During this time, have three boxes, one for giving, one for saving, and one for disposing. Especially when it comes to clothing, anything that has not been used for a year should be donated or thrown out. Being as it has not been used for this long, more often than not, it will not be used any time soon.

As a general rule, everything that has been placed in any of these boxes can no longer be taken out, unless it is the one for saving. All items for donation and disposal should be taken care of accordingly. The minute the cleaning has been done, call respective agencies to assist with these. Donation facilities, the Salvation Army, and similar agencies offer pick-up services depending on the area.

These tips for cleaning and organization will help homeowners maintain their shipping container homes with ease and maximize the amount of space that they have both inside and outside the house. As an added bonus, these habits will also help ensure that the steel structure and all other components of the home are well taken care of allowing it to stand the tests of time and last for years on end.

Advanced Shipping Container Homes

Shipping container homes can come in more complex, advanced forms rather than typical single-storey minimalist housing. The beauty of shipping containers is that they can be stacked, put side by side, modified to the liking of the building owner.

Multiple-Storey Houses

For homeowners that require something larger than a traditional shipping container home built from a single cargo unit, multiple-storey houses can be built by combining several steel units connected horizontally and stacked vertically. The higher the tiers, the lesser weight it can carry as it will depend on the bottom tiers for support. In this case, it is possible to add additional structural support posts on the lower tiers to ensure that the containers are balanced and can support a significant amount of weight.

In some areas, shipping containers are regularly used to provide affordable residences. Because they can be stacked safely and securely, they can provide plenty of individual living spaces given a small patch of land. (Image from www.treehugger.com)

Storage Warehouses

Because of how they can easily be modified and how easy it is not to mention cheap to maintain shipping container structures, there are business owners that have invested in providing these as storage solutions to those who need additional space for their personal belongings. Different containers of different proportions are normally placed side by side in storage warehouses and offered for rent. The usual customers are those who reside in condominium or apartment units, places which usually come with a limited amount of storage space.

Retail Outlets

Just like multiple-storey residential properties, there are shopping centers in different parts of the world that have been built using shipping containers as their base structures. Similar to the concept applied to shipping container homes, these cargo units are stacked and modified to create rentable shopping spaces. Cheap to construct and easy to maintain, these provide investors with a lucrative source of income. Retailers on the other hand also benefit because of the lower rent expense and unique storefront that attracts more customers to their wares.

Leasable Office Space

Similar to retail outlets made out of shipping containers, there are some investors who also construct working office spaces using these cargo units. When used as offices, these cargo units require special care and follow the process of home construction. Insulation has to be put in, proper cleaning is necessary as well. Priming, painting, and sealing of the units is also important.

Dormitories

As a way to make affordable housing readily available for university students, plenty of educational institutions have also started utilizing shipping containers to create makeshift dormitories in various schools across the world.

Because of the standard size of a typical cargo unit, a single shipping container can be used to house two to four students on average. They provide ample space for beds, desks, and common areas and are usually stacked atop one another to as high as five storeys on average.

The great thing about shipping containers is that they can also be used to build retail outlets that are unique. Aside from the stores and their wares, the one-of-a-kind look of container malls add to the appeal for shoppers. (Image from www.inhabitat.com)

As the market for shipping container homes grows and as more of these units are fabricated not only to handle cargo but also to satisfy the purpose of providing ample shelter, many more styles for advanced shipping container homes can be expected in the years to come.

The Future for Shipping Container Homes

As the use of intermodal shipping containers for various architectural purposes continue to gain popularity, there are plenty of things that people can look forward to when it comes to the future of shipping container homes. Many predict that more people will opt for this type of housing for its sustainability and cost-effectiveness while others do so for the unique aesthetic benefit that cargo unit homes provide. In terms of commercial exposure, a number of pop-up container malls have been seen around the world from Europe to South Africa and similar structures, now of a more permanent nature, are underway across Asia and the United States.

Boxpark, the London-based pop-up shopping complex is the first of its kind. It was made entirely out of shipping containers and influenced the trend of shipping container malls across the European nation and United States. (Image from edition.cnn.com)

In 2011, Boxpark officially opened in London although it was for a limited time only. Boxpark is the pop-up retail complex made entirely out of shipping container units each one designed to cater to a particular brand. It is said to be the first of its kind and was built on a temporary location. All shipping containers used for this shopping complex were recycled. Boxpark revolutionized the retail industry in Europe as it offered real estate developers and businesses alike with an alternative to the old concept of malls, which most people are slowly outgrowing. Not only are they changing shopper attitudes but the concept has given attention to the need to go back to horizontal commerce; providing retail products and services at eye-level.

Boxpark was strategically located along East London's high fashion Shoreditch High Street by a vacant lot in the area. Boxpark was created by using sixty recycled steel shipping containers all of which are of the twenty foot standard size. The shipping containers were arranged to form five rows and were stacked to only have two levels. It took Boxpark's creators a year to finish construction for the pop-up project. The man behind it is a well-known British businessman by the name of Roger Wade. Wade is the entrepreneur that established the Boxfresh fashion label that earned him his fortune back in the nineties.

When he created the Boxfresh brand, he sold his wares in any market he could find. As he spent time in these stalls, he focused on international shipping starting with Hong Kong. He has always had this fascination with shipping containers and loved the idea that it could be used for more than just a transport container. By setting up Boxpark, Wade was able to achieve something that was closely associated to his dreams of international commerce right in his hometown.

Boxpark was a temporary retail complex but was given an initial lease of five years; enough time for the developers and retailers to prepare the next shipping container pop-up. Aside from satisfying the demand for rebirthed horizontal shopping experience, the concept allowed for an environmentally friendly not to mention sustainable structure. There were more benefits to it than just a different kind of shopping experience.

It is this sustainability and reduced carbon footprint that heightened its appeal and continue to encourage support from patrons around the world. The same concept was brought to South Africa and smaller varieties have been seen in different parts of the globe, most of the time built by specific brands for special events or product launches. A popular brand that continually makes use of the shipping container retail pop-up is Doc Martens.

Part of the structure's sustainability, aside from its use of recycled shipping containers, is the fact that it holds no special form of insulation or internal components. Its insulating technology is fairly simple with everything from the utilities to the electrical aspects powered by a series of solar panels. It is not only the first of its kind when it comes to revolutionary complex structure but is also the first of its kind when it comes to energy efficiency in a commercial environment. Boxpark reduces carbon emissions from its daily operations and also lessened internal or embodied carbon emissions as it was built with recycled materials. There was no need to expel energy to manufacture the materials needed for it to come to fruition.

The architectural concept that started with modular shipping container homes are now being adopted into a more complex form of urban housing. There is a popular game where the player stacks housing blocks with the goal of achieving as high of a stack as possible without the building collapsing. This is being brought to life by a team of architects and engineers from Europe. The concept is for stackable and movable apartments.

Pre-fabricated shipping container homes, fully furnished and ready for occupancy, are stacked atop one another via a heavy-load crane. (Image from realestate.yahoo.com)

The common terminology for this residential complex is the pop-up apartment. Basically, the concept is a cluster of prefabricated tiny homes and they have been named Y Cubes. Each Y Cube can be stacked atop the other. So far, its creators are planning on achieving 10 storeys per complex. They are intending on building prefab homes strong enough to handle twenty to thirty stacks without having to apply additional support beams on the lower tiers. Aside from being able to stack these studio apartments, the design is also meant to allow the developers to dismantle the homes, when necessary. Dismantling means removing a stack or two and repositioning them in other locations or other building complexes.

Each unit has a bedroom, living area, kitchen, and bathroom all fitted into 280 square feet of open space. The open plan living area allows for a maximized use of space. The beauty of the Y Cube is that each one comes with its very own deck area. The appearance is pretty simple but basic aesthetics work best when it comes to this apartment complex. The streamlined look allows for a more spacious external look. Each Y Cube is built in a different location, a factory, where everything from the gas lines, plumbing, and electric connections pre-made into each unit. When it is delivered to its final location by truck and crane, the homeowner simply has to plug it into a preset grid and the unit will be all powered up and ready for occupancy. Because of the stackable pre-fab design, it is easy to add more units to a complex. Each container unit is reinforced with cement and wood to allow each tier to withstand the weight.

The brains behind this project are architects Rogers Stirk Harbour + Partners. Each unit costs $75000 to make and this is extremely cheap compared to how much typical apartments and condominium units go for. Aside from the lower overall cost, these units can also be made at a much faster rate. Initially, the project was meant to provide homes for the increasing homeless population of London where rent is somewhat expensive. The first release consisted of thirty-six units. It was offered for less than half of the average rent charged in the city. Aside from this, payments were staggered enabling homeless renters to comply with the monthly payments. All thirty-six units only took less than half a year to complete. The complex comes with an outer shared yard and playground.

The layout for these movable apartments feature a studio setup. (Image from realestate.yahoo.com)

Because of the immense success of the Y Cube project, various developers abroad are considering implementing the concept building more units and positioning them across Europe. Other developers are also considering using the Y Cube concept to create middle to high-range residential options for urbanites. The Y Cubes are meant to offer housing to the needy for a five-year period while the latter is meant to offer permanent housing for sale that can be moved from location to location when needed. It gives a completely new definition to relocation.

What once was a time when homeowners need to leave their abode in search for greener pastures, or a better backyard, now involves a simple appointment with a crane and shipping company. With the urban cubes, homeowners can move their entire residence to any city of their choosing with ease. To make this possible, developers are planning on having cube complexes around the world. If a homeowner needs to move, for as long as a slot is available, their shipping container home can be squeezed into the slot and voila!

As the popularity of shipping containers used for residential and commercial space provisions continue, the architectural community expects the creation of a series of creative buildings inspired by the imagination. With the continued use of recycled shipping containers comes the hope of the development and improvement of building materials that are sustainable in nature. The future sees more of these things being readily available across global markets at prices that are more affordable.

Conclusion

There are different things that potential homeowners planning on investing in shipping container homes have to know before taking a leap on this type of structure. It is important that each and every one of these be understood so that they know what they are getting themselves into and they will be fully prepared for the construction aspect allowing them to prevent any mishaps and avoid any costly mistakes during the build.

Aside from windows and entryways, a number of builders also make use of shipping container units to create makeshift deck spaces for residential container complexes. (Image from edition.cnn.com)

Before construction even begins, ample research is very important when it comes to shipping container homes. Finding a source for units, new or old, is extremely crucial. Checking to see if units are up to standard in terms of strength, wear, and cleanliness should not be ignored. Significant time and effort should also be spent looking for the right laborers from contractors to architects and builders if the homeowner will choose to outsource work for the project.

Apart from the initial construction, ample planning is also required when it comes to the design element of the project. Given that shipping container homes offer enough but limited internal space to work with, homeowners should find ways to make their daily lives efficient may it be in the type of furniture that they use to the functions that they assign to each area in the home. In this case, the best approach would be to get the assistance of an expert interior designer.

There are plenty of available designs, plans, and influences that can improve the overall plans and resulting outcome for projects using container units may they vary in scale and purpose. Mixing and matching existing ideas, and injecting one's own sense of imagination, is an excellent way of coming up with a residence that can be made one's own.

In the long run, a standard shipping container home can rake up huge savings for the homeowner easily allowing him or her to have the funds necessary for a more advanced shipping container home project. Given that the homeowner enjoys the benefits that this type of home can provide, he or she can engage in multiple-storey builds next or better yet, influence or encourage friends and family to try this type of home structure for themselves. As the niche market for shipping container homes grow, so does the market for sustainable housing across the world.

Shipping container homes can easily provide a unique abode to those who are interested in a sustainable form of shelter. It boasts numerous features from hassle-free construction to simple planning while offering a wonderful housing option at a fraction of the cost of traditional homes. Although there are several challenges or hurdles as it may that come with the construction of this kind of house the resulting outcome and the benefits that come with it surely overcome them.

22644112R00067

Printed in Great Britain
by Amazon